COEUR DE LION

CŒUR DE LION

ARIANA REINES

FENCE BOOKS

First published by Mal-O-Mar, November 2007

Published in the United States by Fence Books, Science Library 320, University at Albany, 1400 Washington Avenue, Albany, NY 12222, www.fenceportal.org

Fence Books is a project of Fence Magazine, Incorporated, which is funded in part by support from the New York State Council on the Arts and the National Endowment for the Arts, along with the generous sponsorship of the New York State Writers Institute and the University at Albany. Many thanks to these friends and to all Friends of Fence.

Fence Books are distributed by Consortium Book Sales & Distribution (cbsd.com) and Small Press Distribution (spdbooks.org), and are printed in Canada by The Prolific Group (prolific.ca)

Design by Ariana Reines. "Coeur de Lion" cheese photograph by Sinan Sevimli.

Library of Congress Cataloguing in Publication Data
Reines, Ariana
Coeur de Lion/ Ariana Reines

Library of Congress Control Number: 2011937667

ISBN 13: 978-1-934200-48-3

SECOND EDITION
Second Printing
10 9 8 7 6 5 4 3

The other night
When I couldn’t sleep
Next to you and I
Said I wanted to cry
And you said I should
And I looked down and breathed
And then I did cry
And you tried to touch me
And you did
And you tried to kiss me
And you sort of did
And I was so scared
That I love you and you don't love me
I felt stupid when I put my pants on
And I felt stupid when I put my shirt on
And I felt stupid when I went to the other room to get my book
Beware of Pity by Stefan Zweig
The preamble to which I had read to you
When I still thought we might fuck
And I felt stupid when your door
Slammed too loud behind me
But when I hit the night air
I was relieved.

You read a lot. You have a hunger.
I like it. Your hunger makes
It possible for you to see things.
You must have seen how stupid I felt
How helpless.
Women.
I don't know, Jake.
I do not understand women.
Right now I feel like one.
I don't know what women want
But I know that the ones I like
Are not the hags
Who put one arm around you
(In this scenario you
Are the younger woman)
And say *You get to a point in your life.*
Fuck those bitches
Who try to poison desperate girls
With their resigned and shitty worldviews.
Women. They have got to feel desire.
Me too. I've got to feel it.
And your ex, or maybe you're back with her
I don't know, Emma. I read some of what she wrote
To you when I broke into your gmail account.
She's charming. A little shallow maybe

But clever. Undemanding, I guess.
We are not very alike; you are sweet
And condescending when you write to
Her. It is difficult to know
Anything. I guess she seems
Lovely. She has curly
Hair like me, but in this jpeg it looks like
She puts more emollients in hers.
You call her Bunny.
That's cute. Sometimes
When I am straddling you, you
Say this ridiculous thing, *Mama*
Llama. Sometimes you whimper
And moan and pretend
To cry, you say, Oh
Ari, you make me feel
So many emotions.
I felt a lot of emotions too.
I think that I do not like the girls
Who apologize like children
If they ever act uncute.
Sometimes I apologize. I
Apologized to you. Too bad
I'm not stronger. I'd be worse.
Emma works at a gallery

One floor down from a gallery where
I worked like three years ago.
She is the Gallery Girl.
I know what that's about.
I was the Gallery Girl. I tried
To like it. It was important
To pretend to be interested
In being near artists and art
As though proximity were tantamount
To metonymy, which it isn't, not in real
Life. What's metonymy
In real life. You rub up
Against something; some of its
Truth and incompleteness
Is transferred onto you;
You carry it around on
Your body. Maybe. Art. That fussed
Trite shit rich people buy.
When I worked upstairs
From where Emma works
I was afraid of what it meant
To exist *alongside* somebody
Else's idea of art. My heart
Was breaking.
I never got good

At affecting the blank expression
Of truly contemporary beauty.
Also I'm weird
Looking. I have used
The words Real; Feel.
When I worked
For the gallery a floor above where
Emma works, I wore miniskirts
And strange dresses, and my boss,
Basically a fake and what the Nineteenth-
Century French called
An *arriviste* (I can be pretentious
Cos I'm talking about the artworld)
Used to introduce me to collectors
As her "genius." Aside from that
Quirk, the strange
Thing about this woman
Was that despite the fact that what she wanted
Was fame and more money (she already had a lot
Of money) she had a curious appetite for ideas.
And adjectives. The thicker the better.
Words. I got to use some in her place
Because some bizarre mental
Excess in her attracted
Her to them. Her insane brother

Fired me three times. Anyway,
I don't know why I'm telling you this
Except that I think Gallery Girls
Have something to do with
What some women want and do and are.
What about Gallery Boys, which is
To say Art Handlers.
They count too. Bleh.
One can try to fall for the idea that sitting
And standing in a room with something in it
Somebody is willing to pay for
Is the same thing as having
A heart; beliefs. The open system
One passes through will find
A way to take effect one
Way or the other. This firm
Notion, a pendant
Of the culture, such as it is.
It felt so lame, picking
Up the phone, acting
Pretty and disdainful
When I'm neither.
Pretending that bullshit's
Something I know how to do
When I'm so bad at it. Too nerdy

And emotional. Too fucking enthusiastic.
Some people can make anything
Sound true. I've been a whore before
Too. Maybe it's cos I always
Want to know
About women that I've done
These degrading jobs.
Some women're so intense
Jake, you know what I
Mean? Intense enough they're never
What they are; never merely.
I don't mean some internet-ready
Self-reflexivity, self-irony, whatever
People call it, as if a self were so fixed
Just ironizing "it" could constitute
A surge of consciousness.
I fall for women
Who are beyond themselves,
You, their situation, and everything.
Those are the women I want to know
About. Those are the women I want to know.
Right now I'm listening to Nico
And considering feeling
Intimidated. I want to feel love.
I loved you when you said

It is horrible what has happened
To Mediterranean culture. And I loved you
When you said what I couldn't have
Tricked you into saying
That it was so much more intense, the sex
And everything between you and me
Than it was between you and her.
I have never been the other girl before.
It makes me sick with dread
But I can't stop myself
From writing to you like this

Abigail called me
After I snuck into your email
To say that you were flipped out
And that initially she was surprised
That I would do a thing like that.
Me and Abigail hung out
We got veggie burgers
And I explained to her
How I was feeling
And she understood.
I was touched that of all people
You would call her
The morning after being
Betrayed by me in this way
Because you are always teasing me
About how much Abigail respects me
Or I think you are teasing me
When you tell me
That she respects me. I respect her
Too. A lot. Maybe I hear
Something derisive in your voice
When you say nice things to me
That isn't there. But I think
That you would agree that something derisive is
There.

I’m starting to feel nauseated

Cos you haven’t written to me

Since yesterday

It bothers me that your family
Is wealthy and that you pay a lot of money
For telephone sex and webcam masturbating

When we watched clips of "Apocalypto"
On YouTube with your friend Mikael
I was surprised at how bored I was by them.
Apocalypto is an awesome title, we agree.
And Mel Gibson is like some kind of grotesque rendition
Of a stupid, stupid Georges Bataille
But his bloodlust, in its excess, is dull.
Its voracity runs too headlong
Into the carnage, or something, it doesn't
Exploit the eros of violent possibility enough.
I told you some things I learned
About Maya bloodletting rituals
From this book called *The Blood of Kings*
Sinan bought for me at The Metropolitan
Museum of Art, another place I used to work.
About how it was kings and nobles, women too,
Who bled themselves in order to have visions.
They pierced their shins, their tongues, their foreskins
With lancets made of stingray
Spines and they
Bled into special bowls
Of paper.
The paper soaked up
The blood.
A vision came out of the blood.

The vision is usually depicted
As a serpent, well, the serpent
Comes out of the blood and in the serpent's
Open mouth is the vision itself.
The noble people
Who bled themselves in front of
The common people
Were supposed to bear their pain
Stoically. One relief shows Lady
Xòc passing a thornèd rope
Through the bloody hole in her tongue.
As it fell the blood was rubbed
Into the stone hieroglyphs on the walls
Of the temple and cos
Everything's a hieroglyph in that
World, it's impossible to separate
Blood, architecture, figuration, and
Pain from language itself.
This is really interesting, you said.
I played "Let My People Go," by
Diamanda Galas for you.
This is the shit, you said.
I guess I was trying to call
Your bluff—what you'd
Said about me being witchy

And everything.
That night I had called you
Because I wanted to see you
And you were very amenable;
You got beer.
Your apartment is conveniently located.
It took some courage for me to call you
Because you'd been kind
Of distant and I saw the effort
You were making to be pleasant
With me while you tried to figure
Out what you wanted; how best to
Nudge me in that direction.

I want to write you
About my perfidy
And I am scared to.
I feel so much for you that I can’t talk to you.
According to you I ruined
“Things” and turned you “into
A monster” but whatever.
I saw Sinan today. The sun was hot
And he looked so louche. He was smoking
A Nat Sherman.
They are great for rolling joints, he said.
I felt very human.
We talked about ambition.
I thought about you and how scary it is
The way you keep your distance
And I thought about the cherishing feeling
I sometimes have for you.
Thinking about a person. Surely
That act releases something
Into the atmosphere. A toxin?
Now that I am not addressing you
But the “you” of poetry
I am probably doing something horrible and destructive.
But this “I” is the I of poetry
And it should be able to do more than I can do.

I think it would make me uncomfortable
To have poems address themselves to me.
I think that it is old-fashioned
A kind of aggressive defacement
The love poem.
But you are so good at handling
Uncomfortable situations
Maybe the quantity of inspiration
Ha, another old-fashioned word
That's installed itself in me ever since we got together
Will be something you could
Eventually be okay with

When we lay down
In Venice
On the patio of the restaurant
That was closed
And hid behind the chairs and tables
With the night people passing by
It was lovely
You fucked me
You came somewhere on me
I had a painful zit on my upper lip
And we were covered in dust
From the stones of Venice
I photographed a broom
And indecipherable monograms
On the walls of Venice.
You told me your story.
The story made me
Tired and sad.
I have had enough, I said.
We were outside San Giorgio
Maggiore. Can I finish
The story, you said later. OK
I said. I wanted to show
That I could be a hospitable
And generous person.

It was bright and hot.
Discussing interpersonal
Relations makes me tired and
Feel like an asshole. I really
Liked you.

The day after

We first had sex

I had a soft and complicated feeling.

I put a condom on you, and then we took it off.

You fucked me without it, and I liked you.

I remember what you looked like as you undid your things.

The condom stayed on my bedside table

For the length of our stay in the hotel.

The day after our first night

I had a beer with Hannes.

I had sex with Jake, I said.

How do you feel about that, he said.

I don't know, I said.

I don't know.

When we were in the mountains
We straddled a big fallen tree.
I was happy.

It bothers me

That you cut out

American Apparel advertisements

And tape them to your bedroom wall.

The night before the day
That you licked my pussy
And I sucked your cock
By the big fallen tree
I took a walk with John.
The sky was full of stars.
We walked around the valley.
We got to a point.
The night was cool
And thick. We stopped
And kissed. It was nice.
When we got back to his
Room, he took his shirt
Off and I took my shirt off.
We kissed more.
"I think I'm going to go," I
Said. I made some kind of excuse.
"You don't want to have
A sleepover?" he said, "We could
Just hold each other." I went
To my room and dyed my hair.

I don't like it when you say Take Care

When I take my leave of you.

You are writing a book called *Mein Cock.*
It is about your love affair
With a phone sex operator, among other things.
When you told me the story of you
And the phone sex operator
I was moved. After you read
Me about fifty pages of your novel, *Humble*
Monster, and I told you it was "a terrible novel"
(I did not mean to say it like that)
I explained some things
That I did like about it, some things
I thought could be reworked. And
I said that I hoped
That you would write the story
Of you and the phone-sex operator
How good she was at cocksucking
How shitty her life
Was, her poverty, fucked-up
Family, how she hated her
Body, the love you shared.
I felt for her, and you spoke
About her with such elegant
Forthrightness.
The week after school ended
And I was in Germany with Sinan

I got obsessed with Nazi architecture
And started to read *Mein Kampf* online
Until I got blocked by the authorities.
I told you all about it in an email
On August 30th and I feel
That perhaps I am somewhere in some
Small way a part of what has inspired
You to write this book *Mein Cock.*
On the other hand I think your prose
Is sometimes shaky, and following Hitler's
Might not be the best idea.
I guess "cock" could stand
For *kampf,* "struggle," which is pretty
Witty, or could be, but who knows
Where you're going to go with
That. It's really none of my business.

You told me the other night
That you Googled yourself
And found a boring YouTube video
Made by a highschool kid with your
Name. In the video, he said his
Name, you said, and it was so weird.
Somewhere in something
That you sang to me that you had written
This occurred, something about you having
No name, or a name that might as well be no
Name at all. Or no identity. And the dead
Generality of your childhood you'd woken
Up from. I thought of that Nabokov novel
Despair. And Schumann, or was it Schubert?
The Dopplegänger. In any case, I said, How can you read
So much—and you cut me off and
Said, And know so little? and I said
No no. How can you read so much while
You are writing and not become so seduced
In every different direction that you
Betray the thing you're writing?
I do everything in spurts, you said.
When I sent you the mp3
Of "He's a Rebel" by The Crystals
It was because I think you are

A kind of rebel, the kind that I like
The kind who is not afraid
Of what he wants
And who lives in the confusion of it
By reading.
I also sent it
To make fun of you
Because I think your college memories
And father complex are not really much
To rail against, I mean, seriously,
In this world we're living in.

Your arms are brown
And have beautiful veins
That you like. I like your hands.
Your eyes are blue but
Because they need so much light
Your pupils are always dilated and
Your eyelashes are nice. You cannot
Cry but sometimes you whimper as
Though you are crying when
You want to show that you are feeling
Something.
When you shaved your beard
Your mouth was too big
And I liked it.

I forgot all about how
We held hands so tight
All through class but
Then I remembered.
You were writing to Emma
About how much you missed her
And couldn't wait to see her
During this time. I think Emma
Bovary is named Emma
Because of some notion
Of English romanticism, Jane
Austen, something like that.
Emma is not a French name.
I don't remember *Madame*
Bovary that well, but Avital Ronell
Discussed it in her seminar today.
Toward the beginning of the novel
Dumb Charles Bovary's first wife
Dies and Emma's father invites
The widower Charles to dinner.
Emma's father proposes that Charles
Go rabbitting with him, explaining
That shooting a rabbit, "getting off
A shot" or something like that, in Paul
De Man's revision of the translation

By Eleanora Marx, might dissipate
The tensions of his bereavement.
Of course it's not Charles's feelings
Emma's father cares about: He
Just wants to get the transaction
Of his daughter's marriage over with. Anyway
It's a nice name, Emma. And the whole
Shooting a rabbit in order to relax enough
To notice Emma thing and how
You call your Emma Bunny, well
I guess it's kind of a stretch, but
I thought of you two today. I sent
You that VIncent Gallo
Song "Honey Bunny" even though
I knew it would make you think of
Her. Once Abigail called me Bunny
In front of you, I guess cos
I made a face, and
My heart hurt, cos I knew.

When I told you
That Sinan
Is going to Mexico
You said, He stole
Our idea! I said, he stole
MY idea. It is because
I was so moved
That you said "our"
That I could not possibly
Believe you, and anyway,
You *were* joking, weren't you.

There is a bottle

Of tequila

On the table.

I am going to get it.

Did I tell you
That I finally
Read your novel
All the way through?
When I reread
The first few pages
I thought
I might have been
Too hasty
When I told you
That day in the
Valley that
It was terrible but
Then I read on
And it *is* pretty
Bad, not in a
Good way. Sometimes
There is an excellent
Sentence and
My heart swells
With hope—now
That I sort of hate
Myself for having
Fallen for you
("Who are these

Women who fall in
Love with you,"
Someone asks the
Character you named
Humble Monster in
Your novel. "Insane
Bitches," he replies)
You seem like
Such a fop.
But I guess
Fetishizing sentences
Is no fair. They're
Not you. They
Are in your
Vicinity.
Maybe a human will
Always be more
Distressing and absolute
Than what he
Makes.
I hope
So.

The morning after
I definitively ruined
Our relationship
You wrote to me
“Fuck You! The worst
Thing you might confront
In this whole situation
Is my desire to be with you.
That I woke up this morning
And thought about you delicately,
And wanted to be sweet,
And talk to you soon. Fuck
You, Ariana! For making believe,
For being too proud. For reading
Too deeply into words, so much
So that their meaning forms
Into nothing but your insecurities.
Fuck you, for making me say fuck
You to you.”

I love when Racine makes
Phaedra say I LOVE instead
Of I LOVE YOU. She was
Not too proud. It's
Good you had a delicate
Thought. It sucks I ruined
It cos existing made
Me exceed it.
We hadn't fucked
For nearly a week. I felt so
Rejected. During those
Days you wrote exultant
Emails to your girl, something
About, like, the bliss of satiating
Yourself inside her, etc. Even if
I did misprise a bunch
Of it, there was nothing passing
Between us, during that time,
Nothing visible
Not even
Words

When

You jack off all day

Do you ever visualize

Yourself on the planet?

Do you ever feel pinned

Down geographically when you fuck

Do you ever feel so

Singular, an emergency

Never more precisely

Enormous or tiny

As who and what

You are? In exact

Proportion to yourself

As huge as your limitedness

Will let you get, no excess,

And in the midst of so much

Sensation you could break

Apart? Not just from the feeling

But from the terrible

Knowledge?

Does sex ever make

You feel so specific

And alone, Jake, that your heart

Could break?

There's a girl
I used to fuck until
Her pussy got
Destroyed and it
Freaked me out cos
When I touched it
It felt like a tattered
Flag in a puddle.
I asked you if you'd
Ever felt a destroyed
Pussy and you said
No. When I let
This gross man
Stan put his skinny thing
Up my ass and take
Photographs of it
I made $500 in twenty
Minutes but then I
Threw up. I had to
Keep the letter O
In mind because his
Dick felt like
A piece of shit.
I did it a few
Times when I was

Eighteen. My hole
Is just another
Hole in the world
I said in my head
My hole is just
Another hole
In the world.
After a while it
Wasn't that
Bad. But sometimes
Still when somebody tries
To fuck
Me in there I
Cry

When you played "Is This
What You Wanted" and "Field
Commander Cohen" on the stereo, it was
Nice. I played you some Arthur
Russell and you downloaded
His album "World of Echo" off
iTunes. We arrived at an agreement
About Nabokov. I've gone back
And forth about him. He's my mom's
Favorite, so that means there's something
Ingrained in me, whether I want it or not.
You and me agree that everything
About him just wishing he was Joyce is
Unfair. We put it like
This: He was doing his own thing.
I do love the game Ada and Van Veen
Play with the light under trees, and we
Love the description of the puddle
That opens *Bend, Sinister.* I did love
Pnin when I read it. For you, Nabokov is the figure
Of the writer from a wealthy family whose
Youth was not deadened by extremist
American capitalism. You used to be jealous
Of him. Me too, not that I was ever rich
Like you. His childhood

Was the best. My mom was obsessed
With it. It made her very ambitious
In her sensitivity, before she totally
Fell apart. I was happy that through
Nabokov I could talk to you about
Her without crying or feeling too
Scared to. Dear Leonard Cohen sang that
Line that goes *To live in a house that is*
Haunted by the ghost of you
And me. I kept on dreaming
Of houses during the weeks I slept
Next to you, I don't know
Why. Houses, and that Eagles
Song "Take it Easy," which must have come
From your subconscious, not mine, and which
In hindsight, might have been a kind
Of warning. I slept so well next to you
In August; September was up
And down. So far October has sucked
In terms of that.
I could feel her, Emma,
In you, could feel you shoring up
Your affection and saving it for
Her. Maybe you were saving it
For yourself. You weren't not

Nice to me. But I have never
Met a girl who would rather
Have niceness than something closer.
Dissemblers sometimes
Believe their own sleights
Of hand. I'm so fucking sick
Of you, but that's the real
Me talking, and not the me
Of poetry. Where literature
Is concerned, ha ha, I've still
Got work to do.

Almost every time
You wrote me an email
I attacked it. The first email
You wrote to me, which I
Did not attack, said many
Things, for example, “Oh that
We can touch if only
Briefly through our words,
And steal back behind them
Without leaving exposed edges.
Like the cloaked version of our
Self can appear and vanish,
Leaving but a trace of recognition.
I think your friend Avitall [sic] calls
This greeting. A way of appearing
Within the other, without making
A demand. And that can be the elixir
Which we drink for a few days
At least, traces, and hellos
And shadows of ecstasy,
Or some such, and there
Are always apologies. I love you,
Jake.” When I read this
In Munich while Sinan slept
I missed you. I did not fully

Grasp the sweetness, the errors
In what you wrote. You wrote to me
With this delicacy
Concertedly, and I couldn't take it
Seriously. I mistrusted it but I
Think I also loved it. Maybe I did not
Love it, but I loved *you.* I wrote back
Like this: "Jake, I'm
In Munich. I think I'll visit Dachau
Tomorrow. I barely spoke
For the seven hours we were
In the car. The mountains are stupefying.
That was my explanation. I miss you.
I left you an envelope in the lobby.
I have to go now. Love,
Ariana."

I just read
Something John Perry Barlow
Wrote. He used to write lyrics
For the Grateful Dead. His work
With the Electronic Frontier
Foundation and former career
As a cattle rancher make him into
An intriguing kind of statesman.
What I read was a eulogy for the woman
He loved more than any other. A friend
Is going to his birthday party
Tonight. I don't have the required
Gland to assimilate the Grateful
Dead, but something real must
Have been going on there, and I really
Like John Perry Barlow, a gentleman
And scholar, a man of affairs and
Learning, a short man. I like his writing.
The woman he loved
Cynthia Horner
Died suddenly
On an airplane
In her sleep.
In his eulogy
John Perry Barlow

Describes his happiness
With Cynthia; her boundless
Kindness, tolerance, and sense of fun.
She was a woman
Who was truly *game,* he wrote.
I read another essay by him
On nerve.com about all the women
He loves, and it had lots of
Mystical intelligence in it
And I liked it.
I am such a shitty
Woman.

The words on a page
In an open book
Looked stupid to
Me when I was little
Unless I was right up close
To them. They looked
Weak; barely
There.
It made me nervous
That in order
For words on a page
To have power
I had to be close.
I had to be close.

In the mornings
As soon as you left
I'd turn on this weird weather channel
On the TV in my hotel room
For the ten minutes I had to enjoy
Solitude; get dressed.
The TV showed photographs of the Alps
With a ticker reporting the temperature in the area towns and
Villages. The audio came from a local pop radio station.
Most of the music was unbearable
The worst kind of Euro schlock, you know
What I mean. But one
Morning, they played "Smooth
Operator" by Sade. It made me
Indescribably happy
In a simple way I felt could go
On indefinitely.

There are many
Kinds of transmission
Between people.
Stronger things than sentences.
Liquids, exhaled
Words on top of them.
Where is the "you" of You
Tube. Who is the
You of advertising.
You
Tube's You
Being me isn't enough
For me. What
Is You today. What
Is You to them. A slot. An empty
Envelope. A speaker
Should have to pass
Through everything in the world
In order to dare
To *dare*
To say You. (*I want "you"*
In the plural, or something, wrote
John Ashbery.) Sometimes
Something so intense
Passes between people

And the words still help
Sort of, or it sometimes seems
That way in the moment.
Avoir et Être, to have and
To be. The French language
Is built on this binary. Is what
You say in Googlechat to Emma
Less than what you say to me
In the dark? When do you
Decide you're talking to
Literature too? It's hard
To separate a body from
The words it lets fall.
And then the difference
Between what's written
And what seems, outside
Of writing, almost just *to be.*
Writing has to do with
Time. It comes very close
After. Or
It can. This is very
Close after.
So close that it could
Scare me. I hope it
Will. I really hope it will.

This morning you wrote
Back to me. You said that
What really fucking pissed
You off was that I seemed
To have made a “whole project”
Out of reading your emails,
And that I ran through the whole
Devastating thing with “relish.”
It’s true, I did make a project
Out of it. Right now
I’m listening to Stevie Wonder
Sing “Ma Cherie Amour.” I fucking
Love Stevie Wonder. I could fall
In love with him a hundred times.
I know what he means when he says
La La La La La La.

I don't know

What happened.

I know

You wrote

You were fucking me cos

You hated me. That's fair.

I hated you too.

At first.

But by the time you wrote

That you were fucking me cos

You hated me and that I was

A pretentious gypsy Jewess goth

In whose jaw you had gotten stuck

We were saying I love you.

I love words

Cos they're so weak

(repeat)

Do you remember
When I asked you
If you wanted to meet me
In the bathroom
In forty minutes?
I watched you out the window
I saw you leave the classroom
And go into the other building
Where the bathrooms were.
I was wet and happy. White
Clouds had installed themselves
Upon the mountain.
When I finally got away
From Alain Badiou, who was
Explaining something
About set theory and making his obscene laugh
That strange ejaculation that comes out of his mouth
When he speaks as a man who is sure that he is right
And he sticks his long tongue out and nearly gasps
My heart was beating.
We went into the stall
And you slammed me against the wall
And everything was possible

Your cock grew in my hand

And I sucked it

And you came

I guess there is no point saying
These things we did. We know
What we did. But stating them
Is like reinstating them
Inside me. It causes me some pain.
I want to feel this pain
Cos it helps me remember
Things. I am trying to decide
If the things humans emit
Between themselves
Have any reason. I am trying to decide
If the state of thought
Knows anything about
The intensity I felt
With you. Maybe these poems
Are an excess of certain
Fleeting sensations, and I should
Just, I don't know, get high or go
Out dancing; try to make
Something of myself. Even now
As I look at them, and it hasn't even
Been a week, you aren't very clear
In my mind at all and I have no idea
What I miss or what I want, if
Anything. It is so over

Between us, I guess. I see your face
Receding into coffee-colored
Light, I see ochres
And resins in a richness that I can only
Imagine tonight. I am writing this
In order to lose you
For my own purposes, a little
More severely than the dissipated
Vacuum that invests interpersonal
Relations in this place
If this even is a place
Tends to allow. Like the climatic
Metaphors you employed
To describe your emotions, as though
They were inexorable, impersonal as
The planet, as though you were a creature, half
Sentient, at the mercy of the elements.
Saying that when your body did something *you*
Did it too's important in terms of ethics. Even if
Your having been a field across which certain things
Transpired sounds good in terms of physics.
I have to ramp
Up the drama of this or I'll be lost.

Fuck those assholes
Who think that there is nothing
To know about love.
I'm nauseous
Cos of the possibility of us attacking Iran
And the hot rain falling right now.
Manhattan is full of white women with
Businesslike bodies. It's all
Handheld devices.
If I can't make this feeling right now
For you more personal
The general consensus is going to
Fucking kill me. Recall manual
Figurations. Recall metaphors
Of hands. Recall your hands.
My total impotence
As an individual. My failure
At freedom
Of speech. I'm already
Forgetting your face
So maybe I was playing
Myself more than I thought
About having more feelings than
Most assholes.
Liberty.

I don't have to to pay attention
To all the things that're destroying
My existence. The ultimate
Is gradually accomplished
Whether I watch or not.

Jake, when do you think
Save Our Souls
Become a massive advertising campaign
To save the planet.
When did human life finally
Not mean shit anymore really
And don't say anything about Nietzsche
Or what he would say about today's ecology
Or do if you can. If you want.
Speaking of saving the planet
Is like daring to say you to a person for whom
You haven't heaved up your whole
Being in order to approach.
Condescension does not
Begin to describe it.
As though the planet were a trinket
Or money
Or even a species
As though any of the things we are
Could be without the form
Of the globe to give them form
As though the diverse morphologies
Of our terrestrial systems
And their aberrations
Their singularities

Could have anything like sense
Without a planet.
I do not think the absurdity
Of this shift is purely
Ecological. I am a little world, wrote
John Donne. The world
Is gone, wrote Paul Celan.
But the planet, what is it
That assholes speak of saving it
Like they speak of saving Africa
By shopping. Saved.
Saved.
An agate marble
At the bottom of a toilet. A tapioca
Bubble. Our pleasure
As a ball. Donne
Again.
Mein Herze (my heart) wrote
Johann Sebastian Bach
Schwimmt im Blut (swims
In blood). A heart requires
The globe. There is no weather
On the Internet. How, Jake.
HOW DARE THE INTERNET
REFUSE TO CONVULSE.

Wal-Mart has no weather
Either. A heart
Can be replaced.
I fell for you. It felt
Like falling. It always
Does. Now I forget
What you look like
Kind of; I don't remember
What, through or across
You I thought I could
Reach.
I am erecting "you" like a real
Artist. If you read this
You will hate me
Probably. I think you
Are just pretty enough
Just dumb enough
To be my muse.
Cheese, too, has
A heart.
You are so rich, I mean, so brilliant.
I think it does not matter what I think.
I don't know why
You sat down next to me
And grabbed me

In the first place.

I don't know why that night

You shoved money in my face.

I don't know why the next night

I looked at you and said something

About accepting your psychic powers

And when you were strangling

Me and kissing me

I thought it:

I accept.

I accept.

Did you say something
To me on the mountain
About *The Lion King*?

Richard the Lionhearted
Was born in 1157 in Oxford
Where your nice girlfriend or
Ex girlfriend went to college.
"Like most of the Royal
Family at the time Richard
Was essentially French," says
Wikipedia. The word "essentially"
Is curious; strong. Richard grew
Up in France, and, according
To themiddleages.net, spent only
Six months of his ten-year reign
In England, claiming it was "cold
And always raining" there. Your
Girl is British and I am American
Though it is possible that I
Am "essentially" French.
Richard was called
The Lionhearted for his military
Exploits; he was also very
Tall. It does not seem
Unfair to note here that he
Wrote poetry. He never learned
English. Some sources
Suggest it was a desire to be

Memorialized in verse by
Troubadours that attracted
Him to the Crusades. Others
Speak of a deep spiritual
Need. Now remembered if
At all as the crusader held for ransom,
The absent father figure in the Disney
Robin Hood cartoon, the historical Richard was no
Friend of the Jews, even before
He took up the cross: "When
A rumour spread that Richard
Had ordered all Jews to be killed,
The people of London began
A massacre. Many Jews
Were beaten to death, robbed,
And burnt alive. Many Jewish
Homes were burned down
And several Jews were forcibly
Baptised. Some sought sanctuary
In the Tower of London, and
Others managed to escape."
When I was reading your email
Account, I noticed a curious
Motif, a certain derision
About Jews, especially female

Ones, in your messages to
Emma. I thought it was cute
Though, the way she called you
Rabbi, since you teach at a
Yeshiva and everything.
When we were lucky enough
To be in Venice together
Me because of my Stafford loan
And you because of your
Skill trading stocks and commodities
Or maybe because of the backing
Of your family, I don't know,
I enjoyed the things you said
About Palladio and the Renaissance
Even though orderly experiments
With perspective aren't my thing
I'm more into Paolo Uccello; the
Ghetto. I told you about the red
Stone of the Strasbourg Cathedral
And that I feel a heat from Gothic
Buildings that feels so human, like
Geometry and plants fucked each
Other and went insane.
Maybe this is why
You called me a goth? Whatever.

When a person goes
Far away, to an old place
A person is trying to feel
Something about a world
Being possible.
It is easier to fall
In love far away from everything
Familiar. As I write this
There is still a planet.
You have a daddy
Complex and I have
A mommy complex. We do
Not want to fuck the Venus
Of Willendorf. You were into
Saying that I have an obscene
Smile. The morning
After our first night you told
Me my pussy smells good,
Like Swiss cheese. That grossed
Me out, cos I'd thought
It smelled more like unripe

Apples. But then we talked
About the strange carnality
Of cheese; fermented things, how they're
More unsettlingly animal, somehow,
Than animal flesh. In Venice
I bummed a cigarette from a cute
Italian girl and I watched you put
Your fork into an assortment
Of cheeses. I tasted one
And it was so strong I thought I'd faint.
There was wine. You paid for most
But not all of it. That fancy quince
Paste, olives too, how could I forget.
The moon was very big. I felt
Tired and exposed but
Brave. We both said it was good.

I feel the symptom expanding in me. I feel
It expanding into facts.
This nectar oh I have to close my eyes
This is the heat that is too complicated.
Where is Pergolesi
In the availability
Of recorded sound
Where are you when I am going insane
Cos this really is the archive
Not your enormous feelings, but their representation.
I am the additive.
Rock of ages
I am the additive.
Putty, monads, I have to say these things
Because I feel like them.
The mommy is wearing her carrot colored hair.
I came out of her.
The days are getting shorter.
She is becoming coquettish in her senselessness.
I smell the fall air, and I feel the feelings, and I have
Got to get out of here.
Mommy will have a pepperoni slice. This is such a nice place
She says. It is a pizza place. It's fine, I say.
The countertenors are saying, they are saying, they are saying
Amen amen amen.

Fructifying sleep, break me in.
Beasts with hairs, lick me.
The age is too intelligent and too fucking dumb.
This is a lyric poem.
Confutatis, maledictis, make me feel the popular emotions.
I am going to shimmer in the slot.
I am going to dip the mommy in glair.
She comes to me in my dream and speaks
To me of excellence. I should think more
About trappings, connections, says the dream
Of my mommy. She is walking
Down the street in platform sandals
And a silk blouse, my jeans.
The man with bandaged legs
Who lives in a wheelchair on the sidewalk
Wraps his dressings in Duane Reade bags
When it rains. The mommy goes unto him
And gives him money in real life.
The mommy offers me some of the lemonade
I bought her. Sakharov, she says,
Did not suffer the way I suffer, but it will all
Be over soon. She
Is sexually terrifying. Her elegance
And intelligence dignify the insanity so
Much I forget not to be charmed

When she trips over her excessive
Shoes, every day she walks ten miles
In them, and makes an aristocratic
Apology about lost contact lenses, no
Depth perception, and laughs like
She's at a ball. She does not
Want to hurt anybody.
It will take her long
To die and it is impossible
To give her anything. I gave her
Nine dollars, a piece of pizza, and a Snapple
Lemonade. She gave birth to me. Gratitude's
Stupid, an economy I am too desperate to enter
Into. She is becoming stupid. Dave is reading
Demian by Hermann Hesse. I am happy
That he is reading something other
Than the *Tao Te Ching,* cos his lassitude
Sometimes seems sacred and absolute; it scares
Me. I guess cos mine's so weak in comparison.
Where are the messy women who love the fragile boys.
Where are the suicides who are my heroes.
Where are the bitches who know what they want
Who love what they do, bosomy and declarative,
Happy to be artistic in this stupid night.
If something aspires only to resemble itself

Then what the fuck does that mean.
I cannot have sex with pure ambition.
Some tiny sign amplified beyond recognition
Is not enough to be art to me.
A bicycle's not a revolution
Though it revolves and helps.
Synecdoche. I'm tired. This quandary.
I can say that this is the sanctifying privacy
In which I know the day of wrath
The Dies Irae
Should be my sacred everyday
And even is. I said the words
Sanctifying and Sacred; Revolution.
I said the word Art.
The mommy is rinsing her face
In the filthy light of Tenth Avenue and
Forty-Seventh Street: tourists, signage
And sin that's basically unavailable
But extra lurid, for some reason, cos absent.
The sin's these fucking hos in sequined dresses
Performing having it all.
They go to the gym, their haircuts are very current.
They are looking for love and they are walking
Through the present like it is theirs, like they
Believe, and it *is* theirs, cos they believe.

The mommy rinses her eyes in this light.
I am Travis Bickle.
Her mind dips into the agar-agar
The air feels like, her mind dips into
It and sticks. The city's so general
How can she possibly specifically *be*.
These people who are going to have a good time
Are everywhere; up
To date. Day of wrath, burn
Me. Burn me. Hildegard,
Make the voices of the women
Soar up so high. I am listening.
The voices carry
Me. The stony heights
Echo the voices, the air
Is being caressed by them.
Something burns in this sound
The fire's soft and even
Like the oblong flame of my mommy's orange wig.
Is it tiring to be in the closed
System of another person's mind? I am guilty
Of making my associations, of these feelings
Belonging to me when nothing does except the murk
Of where I am located, what information can be harvested
From "my" comings and goings, and the imperfect

And embarrassing things other people probably
Think. Just the facts,
Ma'am. The recorded sound
Of the psalterion
The women singing enormous vowels
I want to feel them sweep over me
And all of this particularity
Fall away. I think it is possible
To be impersonal without being so general
You're dead. I do not want
To optimize. I want to kiss you and feel
Sorry and kiss you again while the mommy
Slowly loses her reality, an
Abrasion in the heavy ledgers kept by statisticians
And demographers, a wound that will not
Heal. They are not ledgers. They are
Databases. This is my poem. I wish I wasn't so
Lonely in this capability of being devastated by
Her. I wish I wasn't alone in this
Awe of her long errand, even now as it starts
To get dumb, and how unloved
She is, and how broke, opening onto an expanse
Of losses so diverse and endlessly amplifiable
That all narration just congeals. I'm broke
Too. Brokeness is not exactly honesty

But sometimes it gets close.
Somebody stole her computer; when she
Had one dollar she bought with it
An adjustable ring. She is a prizewinning
Medical doctor. The facts suffer,
They suffer and die. I want you so badly
In this feeling of things arising
To populate my need for newness.
Yeah, I feel that too. I even bought
A jacket yesterday, and you said
That it looked cute on me, and I knew
When I bought it with my student loan money
That it was because I was afraid
Of losing you and of getting stranded
Forever, an antique
In the horrific hugeness of my heart beating
So fast, all this potential garnering
Dread, dread and impotence.
The mommy is homeless, she can't even
See. She is hungry but with this dollar
She will buy a cup of coffee. The mommy
Has got to feel capable, she has got
To feel it. This is a nice place, she says,
All they need is a liquor license. The mommy
Never drank when she had something

To live for, half a glass of wine made her blush
And fall asleep. Now she is too poor
To drink, but it's the thought that counts.
People who are capable of speaking
For themselves do not understand
The mute and enormous calculation
I meant to type complication
But calculation is more accurate
The mute and enormous calculation
Cracking open on top of them, consuming
Them and us, no matter what we say.
The mommy is on her way
And I came out of her and am distant
From her, writing poetry. I am capable
Of being a woman of action; desperate
For your love. I have walked the streets
Like her, like Demeter too, this is a poem,
I am allowed to speak of myth,
Fuck you, I am allowed to speak to you.
Intellection's still popular cos it's so
Comforting when badly done. If I
Were larger I could help her and not
Lose you at the same time. I am afraid
To face this dread because I am afraid
That seeing me inside this dread

You will leave me, that you will walk away
And I will be her, and, being her, I will try
To contain myself, become obsessively interested
In wainscotings, the gods in details
Cos I will not have the balls
To kill myself, admit I'm wrong, or demand
A love that may not
Even be "it," which can almost feel
Like suicide, and who in my position
Could possibly tell the difference? Here I am
In my position. A little brown mouse
Has just appeared through a hole
On my "desk." It is cute and I am going
To pretend that I have a fond relationship
With it because my heart is swelling and once
When my heart was swelling and I saw a maggot
It was so much worse for me than this.
To speak of maternity
One must speak of the city
And of love, for something other than
Air, or something upon the air
Makes us cleave to each other
At least sometimes
In the night.
When I see a photograph

Of a place that is familiar to me
The house where I am staying for example
The place always looks strange
And more complete than it feels
As I live inside it. This strangeness
Has to do with the air; the atmosphere.
It's right here. I cannot see
What it is doing to me.
I am afraid of the accumulating
Strangeness of this thing that "it"
Is doing to me and I know I cannot
Help it so I am not afraid. I am afraid
Of having nowhere
To go again, like the times before
When I thought I could save her
By becoming her, when I thought
I could absolve myself of my big
Emotions by humiliating them.
I don't know what I think tonight
But I know where I am
This second lost without you

Sinan came over
Today. Since I have destroyed
My responsibilities I have
Time for these long
Conversations about "us." He looked
Beautiful, Jake. You would have
Thought so. His eyes
Are so big and sincere. Sinan
And I had been exchanging
Fuck you emails all morning.
It's not something we do
Often, but it is a way to bring
Pain out into the open. We
Talked. It was good. I believe
In him. While I was
Falling for you
I did not write to him
Enraptured, I did not tell him
How much I missed him the way you
Did to your girl. When I
Was falling for you
I hardly wrote to him at
All. Sometimes in class
I wrote about you in my
Notebook: a few hundred

Sentences in a tiny
Hand. It was a way to feel
Your presence by extra-
Ordinary, by subtle means. I wrote
About when you said to me
I feel like the girl, and I asked you
What you meant and you said
Attached. I wrote about
How we slapped each other
In the face, and your thumb
On my throat, your red
Mouth, and about
The flies that buzzed around us
That day we took our pants
Off in the valley by the fallen
Tree. This is how it is in the
Wild, you said, and I went ha
Ha, and you said, The
Flies smell our pheromones.
There was even a donkey
Screaming, like Balthazar. You are
As dirty as I am, you said. I was happy.
Although Emma and I might
Share superficial resemblances
(I guess the hair and jobs are

All I can really speak of; I really
Don't know shit about
Her), you and Sinan have nothing
In common at all, nothing except
For me. Up in the mountains I
Wrote about loving your body
And the way you moan when
You fuck, about loving the way
You say Oh my god Oh my god,
And your face goes limp and your eyes
Shine. About being a little jealous
And scared you might be more perverse
Than me. While I was writing what I
Wrote about your and my perversion Slavoj
Zizek paraphrased Freud: "The melancholic
Loses the object of desire while the object
Is still there."

Trying to see the proportional relation
Of one memory to another
One is so strange, and then
To try and see what looms
And doesn't for the other person
Who was there, it gets stranger,
Especially when you've read
His email.
I don't know how people
Understand their lives, measure
Their sensations against "objective"
Or so-to-speak democratic estimations,
Whether people accept the externality
Of events, "events," as things
That happen *to* them. I refuse
To accept some coagulate
Of other people's
Impressions in exchange for this
Privacy, no matter how flawed it is.
This is lyric poetry. It has to be. It has
No other hope. What was it
About you and me that made whatever
Happen to us. In New York
Everything fell apart. What I dreaded
And expected.

But still. Tonight
It is dark and the weather is cooler
Than it's been. It has taken
A while for Fall to break; the global
Warming kept me in summer
Love with you like I was under a
Fermata. Now that the times
Are changing, I feel
Even more for you; or I feel nothing,
I can't tell; it's kind
Of scary. I was sick of thinking
About you this morning but
I was listening to Bob Dylan and Leonard
Cohen in order to think about
You for literary purposes.
When I feel nothing for a person
I get scared I'm losing my humanity
And that turning cold means
My heart's been botoxed; we're
All fucked.
I watched a movie on YouTube
Called *Ladies and Gentlemen, Mister*
Leonard Cohen that was made when
He was still just a poet and only
Famous in Canada.

He's a pretentious little nerd
In it, self-important, teacher's pet wit.
I think that, making music, he became
So much nakeder, much more desperate.
The talent, real, even *pure,* even
Natural, had to ripen in
The artificial man.
Alain Badiou, on the last day
Of his class, said, "Because an event
Is pure rapture, an event disappears
Immediately; it does not exist
Objectively, but only by appearing
And disappearing." This is both
Precise and vague; it is attractive
I guess. I guess since you and me did not
Disappear immediately, it was
Not pure rapture, not in these
Terms, but my smile
Was real each time I swallowed
Your cum. Getting
Fucked by you was great; I could
Feel it in my organs, but
You didn't make me go insane
Except for maybe once
Or twice. Actually maybe I am

Being unfair. Maybe the fucking really
Was that great. In this moment I
Can't remember.
I just read a poetry
Review in which the reviewer
States that a certain book
Made his cock feel as though
It were tall as a tree. That's
Nice. I have no idea
What it feels like to have
A cock. Sometimes I feel
As though I'm getting close
To understanding and then
Something happens to make
Me have no clue again. When Sinan
Fucks me, we lose our individuality
So severely it's like we're both
Gasping after an animal that's his
Cock that is beyond us and I lose
All sense of the world. His cock's
Not even him, and he's not him either
And we aren't anything.
It's strange, the possessive. Didn't Thomas
Mann write a book called *Herr*
Und Hund or something like that?

Man's best friend. What belongs
To him. Me and Sunder
Talked about how scary and arousing
It is to watch men masturbate, cos
Everyone relates differently to *his.*
Like dicks are always almost but never
Quite another. *Je est un autre,*
Said that brat Arthur Rimbaud.
I am definitely in love with you
As I write this. You are so petty
And superfluous I cannot stand
You. Sinan is definitely
In love with me. I know, because
I saw him tonight. I love
Him too. You are gracious
To accord me the space and time
In which to develop, or to elaborate
Upon, as the French say, these
Extreme emotions I am, despite
The odds and certain lapses,
So capable of feeling.
It was good to slap
Your face and to admit
That your asshole
Made me nervous.

Your eyes had a way
Of going soft and shiny
When you said the really
Tender things. We admitted
It was intimidating
For us both to hear each other describe
People we've fucked and been
In love with. I'm proud of what
We accomplished together. Alain Badiou
Ended his class with a reading
Of "Ariane et Barbe-Bleue" which
Is an opera by Paul Dukas. You
And me had gone pretty far
By the time this day came, and
Something very fragile in me breaks
When somebody says my name, or
Even a variant of it. I was tired.
I think Badiou discusses "Ariane"
In *Being and Event* which
I have not read. In class he said
That the story of the opera is
About the relationship between law
And freedom, and that it shows
That the desire for freedom is not
So simple. Ariane experiences an Event

That causes her to demand freedom, Badiou
Said, but she is unable to convince anybody
Else, *any other women* to want freedom; she ends up alone.
She genuinely falls in love with the wicked
Bluebeard at the beginning. Bluebeard
Who previously got women by having a castle
To lock them in. This woman Ariane
Does not have to be taken
By force. When she enters
His castle he hands
Her seven keys, six
Of which he gives her permission
To use, and leaves. She hears the cries
Of his other, imprisoned wives,
Coming from behind a door. So she uses
The forbidden key, releasing them.
Meanwhile Bluebeard is assaulted
By the local peasants, who want
To free Ariane, fearing her fate will turn out like
That of the women who came before her.
But Ariane is already free
In herself, and proves this freedom
By bringing the wounded Bluebeard
Home, caring tenderly for him, and then
Declaring that she's leaving him for good.

By the end Bluebeard's shattered, sobbing,
Bleeding. Ariane
Invites the other wives to leave with her
In a wrenching aria, pleading
With them one by one to taste
With her the freedom awaiting
Them, *The World.* But they all prefer confinement
Even though they had longed
For freedom before Ariane opened
Their door. Once liberty arrived they were no
Longer capable of it, preferring to serve; even a gutted,
Hollowed-out power. Ariane exits
Alone. The end. Badiou narrated
This with emotion and
I cried. Maybe cos I was tired and
That thing about my name or because
I am not heroic or free.
I had missed half of Alain Badiou's
Lectures messing around with you
On the couch by the fire; in the women's
Toilets; up on the hill. If this were a suitable parable,
And it isn't, I would try to tell myself
That those very early mornings in Brooklyn when I sat
Up in your bed feeling wrong and
Got dressed and walked away, I should

Have stayed away cos I don't need you.
Maybe I don't need you. But I want
You. Maybe I don't love you. But
I am getting to know you. Maybe
What made me cry in class was how tired
I was and how sad and hard
It is, and how rare, to undertake an act
That's truly free, and not just a response
To a confused surge of drives and fears.

On August 27th I wrote to my
Friend Emma Wolf that I loved
Fucking you and that you might be
A bad writer, which made me
Nervous. At least he is a stock
Market genius, I said. That really
Makes me feel excluded and
Inferior. Did I mean that? I don't
Even know. Maybe it all comes
Down to lust and dishonesty
Or maybe the only sincere
Things's attraction and repulsion,
Zero and one.
All that medieval love poetry
With its military metaphors
The woman as the fortress
The errancies of gallant knights.
Maybe long ago things were too
Too solid, and now we live in an ether
Of ex-sentiments, impossible
To make sense of except for wet
Panties, something that even
In hindsight might never
Consolidate into a real emotion.
It's been so easy for you

To disengage yourself from your
Behavior, as though you really
Were conjectural, as though
Your desire really were as limitless
And general as the fucking internet.
You keep on saying
That you bear no grudges (our mutual
Friends tell me this) but I really
Wish you would.

You gave me *Toward*

A New Architecture by Le

Corbusier, *The Periodic*

Table by Primo

Levi (I picked

It out) and "Belly

Of an Architect" on DVD. I

Gave you *The Cow* which

Made me nervous and ashamed.

You loaned me *Deep Time*

Of the Media by Siegfried

Zielinski, *Studies in Iconology*

By Erwin Panovsky, *The Freudian*

Body by Leo Bersani, and *Visions*

Of Excess by Georges

Bataille. I've only returned

This last. I loaned you

The Rings of Saturn by W. G.

Sebald, *The Sluts* by Dennis

Cooper, and *Jakob von Gunten*

By Robert Walser. I persuaded you

To buy *Nightwood* by Djuna Barnes and

Michel Houellebecq's *The Elementary*

Particles. I read "A Last World" by John

Ashbery aloud to you. It made

Me blush. My heart was beating.
You told me that an arrangement
You had with your parents
That would soon come to an end
Meant you could still get them to pay
For books. You offered to order
Some through them on my
Behalf. Thank you, I said,
How many? How about six,
You said. We never got
Around to that. It was
Awkward.
I probably should have loaned you
I Love Dick by Chris
Kraus. And Martin Buber's
Tales from the Hasidim; the correspondence
Of Rilke, Pasternak, and
Tsvetayeva. You
Can still borrow those
If you want. I'll want them all
Back eventually. Do you
Want your books back?
You can have them.
Anytime.

COMPAGNIE DES FROMAGES
150g
VIRE FRANCE
PETIT CAMEMBERT
COEUR DE LION
FABRIQUÉ EN NORMANDIE

FENCE BOOKS has a mission to redefine the terms of accessibility by publishing challenging writing distinguished by idiosyncrasy and intelligence rather than by allegiance with camps, schools, or cliques. It is part of our press's mission to support writers who might otherwise have difficulty being recognized because their work doesn't answer to either the mainstream or to recognizable modes of experimentation.

The Motherwell Prize is an annual series that offers publication of a first or second book of poems by a woman, as well as a one thousand dollar cash prize.

The Fence Modern Poets Series is open to poets of any gender and at any stage of career, and offers a one thousand dollar cash prize in addition to book publication.

For more information about either prize, or more information about *Fence*, visit www.fenceportal.org.

The Motherwell Prize

Negro League Baseball	Harmony Holiday
living must bury	Josie Sigler
Aim Straight at the Fountain and Press Vaporize	Elizabeth Marie Young
Unspoiled Air	Kaisa Ullsvik Miller

The Alberta Prize

The Cow	Ariana Reines
Practice, Restraint	Laura Sims
A Magic Book	Sasha Steensen
Sky Girl	Rosemary Griggs
The Real Moon of Poetry and Other Poems	Tina Brown Celona
Zirconia	Chelsey Minnis

Fence Modern Poets Series

The Other Poems	Paul Legault
Nick Demske	Nick Demske
Duties of an English Foreign Secretary	Macgregor Card
Star in the Eye	James Shea
Structure of the Embryonic Rat Brain	Christopher Janke
The Stupefying Flashbulbs	Daniel Brenner
Povel	Geraldine Kim
The Opening Question	Prageeta Sharma
Apprehend	Elizabeth Robinson
The Red Bird	Joyelle McSweeney

National Poetry Series

A Map Predetermined and Chance	Laura Wetherington
The Network	Jena Osman
The Black Automaton	Douglas Kearney
Collapsible Poetics Theater	Rodrigo Toscano

Anthologies & Critical Works

Not for Mothers Only: Contemporary Poets on Child-Getting & Child-Rearing
Catherine Wagner & Rebecca Wolff, editors

A Best of Fence: The First Nine Years, Volumes 1 & 2
Rebecca Wolff and Fence Editors, editors

Poetry

Mercury	Ariana Reines
Cœur de Lion	Ariana Reines
June	Daniel Brenner
English Fragments / A Brief History of the Soul	Martin Corless-Smith
The Sore Throat & Other Poems	Aaron Kunin
Dead Ahead	Ben Doller
My New Job	Catherine Wagner
Stranger	Laura Sims
The Method	Sasha Steensen
The Orphan & Its Relations	Elizabeth Robinson
Site Acquisition	Brian Young
Rogue Hemlocks	Carl Martin
19 Names for Our Band	Jibade-Khalil Huffman
Infamous Landscapes	Prageeta Sharma
Bad Bad	Chelsey Minnis
Snip Snip!	Tina Brown Celona
Yes, Master	Michael Earl Craig
Swallows	Martin Corless-Smith
Folding Ruler Star	Aaron Kunin
The Commandrine & Other Poems	Joyelle McSweeney
Macular Hole	Catherine Wagner
Nota	Martin Corless-Smith
Father of Noise	Anthony McCann
Can You Relax in My House	Michael Earl Craig
Miss America	Catherine Wagner

Fiction

Prayer and Parable: Stories	Paul Maliszewski
Flet: A Novel	Joyelle McSweeney
The Mandarin	Aaron Kunin